First published 1997
First reprinted 1998
This impression 2001

ISBN 0 7110 2548 7

© Derek Penney 1997

Published by Ian Allan Publishing

an imprint of Ian Allan Publishing Ltd,
Terminal House, Shepperton,
Surrey TW17 8AS.
Printed by Ian Allan Printing Ltd,
Hersham, Surrey KT12 4RG.

Code: 0101/3

*Front cover:* 'A2' Pacific No 60532
*Blue Peter* coasts down to Bridge of
Allan with the 1.30pm Aberdeen to
Glasgow express in July 1966.
*All photographs by the author*

*Rear cover:* Awaiting the 'right-
away' at Perth, 'A4' No 60009
*Union of South Africa* is heading an
Aberdeen to Glasgow express.

*Right:* 'A3' No 60082 *Neil Gow*
crosses the Scarborough line
diamonds at the north end of York
station in 1959.

# LNER Pacifics IN COLOUR

## Derek Penney

IAN ALLAN
*Publishing*

# Introduction

The London & North Eastern Railway was alone among the Big Four companies created by the Railways Act of 1921 in operating 4-6-2 Pacific locomotives throughout the whole of its existence, inheriting newly-built 4-6-2s from two of its constituent companies and appointing the designer of one of them, H. N. Gresley of the erstwhile Great Northern Railway, as its first Chief Mechanical Engineer. In the 1920s his 'A1' class Pacifics — and later the 'A3s' and streamlined 'A4s' — established the 4-6-2 as the LNER's preferred locomotive type for the haulage of express passenger services on its East Coast main line and, as the era of streamlined luxury trains unfolded, they earned for themselves an illustrious reputation, and for their designer, a knighthood.

Sir Nigel Gresley's successors continued to build Pacifics: Edward Thompson's radically different 'A2' class mixed-traffic engines lacking the graceful proportions of their forebears; those of A. H. Peppercorn restoring much of the ancestral character. Peppercorn's first Pacific, a new variation of the 'A2' class, was the last to be turned out by the LNER, emerging from Doncaster plant in December 1947. A further 63 Pacifics of LNER design were to be built by British Railways, including the final 'A1' class of express passenger locomotives. Thus, with 202 locomotives comprising eight distinct designs, the lineage of LNER Pacifics was complete by the end of the decade.

In the early 1950s the 'A1s', having proved to be fine engines, assumed many of the more important duties displacing, among others, the war-weary 'A3s', some of which were transferred to the former Great Central line where they became neglected and unloved. Before the end of the new decade, however, the fortunes of the older Pacifics were to change for the better following the introduction of improved methods of construction and maintenance. Later, the fitting of the Kylchap double-exhaust arrangement to all Gresley Pacifics had an especially beneficial effect on the 'A3s' and brought them back into the front rank alongside the 'A4s'. By coincidence, a more ominous development from the viewpoint of the steam enthusiast was the arrival of the first of the English Electric Type 4 diesels and the prototype 'Deltic'.

Those early diesels had little impact on the scene, but delivery of the production 'Deltics' did rob the Pacifics of the cream of their duties on the East Coast main line and clearly heralded their demise. Despite that bleak outlook, for the time being steam was to remain prominent in the mix of motive power and the patchy reliability of the new units meant that the steam enthusiast could not safely ignore even the 'Deltic' workings as Pacifics were often substituted, sometimes completing the impossible-for-steam diagrams. It was the arrival of the all-pervasive Brush Type 4 diesels and the closure of King's Cross Top Shed in 1963 that dealt steam the fatal blow, as large numbers of Pacifics were withdrawn or transferred northwards. As the survivors retrenched they became increasingly employed on secondary duties, or acted as stand-ins for indisposed diesels, instead of being star performers in their own right.

There was, however, to be one last starring role for the Pacifics in the unlikely setting of the ex-LMS Glasgow to Aberdeen line. Exiled King's Cross and Gateshead stalwarts joined surviving Scottish-based Pacifics to give their many admirers north of the Border a wonderful Indian summer of steam working lasting until 1966, and made Scotland a holiday must for others intent on securing a last piece of the action. It was strangely ironic that these veterans of the East Coast route should end their days taking the westward fork at Kinnaber Junction.

Although the immediate prewar era will doubtless be regarded by many as the pinnacle of LNER Pacific achievement, the operational peak was perhaps during the late 1950s and early 1960s when around 200 locomotives were active, some almost 40 years old and better than new. It was around this time that the author, who first came to know these engines in the late 1940s and was to remain a devotee to the end of their days, first recognised the enhanced immediacy afforded by colour film in recording the railway scene and began the collection from which this selection of photographs is drawn. They depict the engines, for the most part in-steam and active, from that operational high noon in the late 1950s to the final swansong seasons in Scotland. The illustrations are arranged loosely in running number order, with ready departure from exact sequence where this is thought to benefit presentation, for the objective is to provide a portrayal, rather than a chronicle, of this celebrated family of locomotives in their final years.

## Bibliography

Cecil J. Allen: *The London and North Eastern Railway*; Ian Allan Ltd
Cecil J. Allen: *Gresley Pacifics of the LNER*; Ian Allan Ltd
O. S. Nock: *The Gresley Pacifics*; David and Charles
Railway Correspondence & Travel Society:
    *Locomotives of the LNER, Parts 1 & 2A*
Railway Correspondence & Travel Society: *The Railway Observer*
P. N. Townend: *Top Shed*; Ian Allan Ltd

*Derek Penney*
*Sheffield*
*February 1997*

## Acknowledgements

The author offers sincere thanks to Derek Huntriss, through whose initial good offices and encouragement this book has come about.

*Right:* A quintessential Grantham scene was that of a Gresley Pacific standing at the southern end of the station with the Lee & Grinling grain warehouse in the background. In mellow afternoon sunshine in April 1959 No 60111 *Enterprise* — the first 'A3' — waits to relieve another Pacific for the last leg of the journey to London.

*Above:* Gresley had introduced his 'A4' class Pacifics in 1935, initially to haul the high-speed 'Silver Jubilee' train, and increased their numbers steadily over the next three years to total 35 locomotives. Of these, only four were fitted with Kylchap blast pipes and double chimneys when first built, but between May 1957 and November 1958 the remainder of the class also had the Kylchap arrangement fitted, with immediate beneficial effect on their freedom of steaming and coal consumption. Notwithstanding these improvements, 'A4' No 60003 *Andrew K. McCosh* was to become one of the first of the class to be withdrawn from normal service, although when pictured at Grantham in the early summer of 1959 the effects of dieselisation had only just begun to cast a shadow over its future.

*Right:* By May 1964, when the long-time Scottish-based 'A4' No 60004 *William Whitelaw* was recorded leaving Perth with the 1.30pm express from Aberdeen, dieselisation had deprived the 'A4s' of their traditional express passenger work on the East Coast main line and the only duties that remained for them worthy of their abilities were these tightly-timed 3hr services between Glasgow and Aberdeen. The name honours the first chairman of the LNER and had been placed on the locomotive when it was first transferred to Scotland in July 1941, having previously been carried by the Gresley 'A1' Pacific No 2563.

*Left:* Rather grubby by usual Top Shed standards, 'A4' No 60006 approaches Grantham with a northbound express in the spring of 1962. Originally named *Gadwall*, it had become the second 'A4' to carry the name *Sir Ralph Wedgwood*; the first had been damaged beyond repair by enemy bombing at York shed on 29 April 1942, only four years after entering service. This 'A4' had better luck, escaping the 1962-3 massacre when 14 out of the 19 King's Cross 'A4s' were withdrawn, and survived in Scotland for another two years.

*Above:* This view of 'A4' No 60007 *Sir Nigel Gresley*, which dates from December 1957, shows it shortly after leaving Retford. The train, which is composed of an entire rake of British Railways carmine and cream-liveried stock, is the 10am from Leeds to King's Cross. The reversed headboard is that of the 'Yorkshire Pullman' which the locomotive would have worked down from King's Cross the previous evening. There is no doubt that the naming after its designer of this, the 100th Gresley Pacific to be built, was a popular and well-deserved tribute, but it did initiate an unfortunate policy trend whereby, down the years, 10 other 'A4s' would have their bird names replaced by those of various LNER dignitaries.

*Left:* Following the successful operation of the prewar 'Silver Jubilee' high-speed service between London and Newcastle, the LNER introduced in 1936 the 'Coronation' and 'West Riding Limited' streamlined trains, the latter of which served Leeds and Bradford. It cut the journey time between Leeds and London to less than 2¾hr. For the inauguration of this service two 'A4s' were specially named *Golden Shuttle* and *Golden Fleece*, reflecting the woollen industry of the area they served. *Golden Fleece* was to keep her name to the end, but *Golden Shuttle* was in 1945 renamed *Dwight D. Eisenhower*, after the Supreme Commander of the Allied Forces in Europe. On a busy afternoon at Grantham in 1962 No 60008 *Dwight D. Eisenhower* is restarting a heavy southbound extra after relieving another Pacific. The locomotive is still cold, as indicated by the white exhaust, despite the hot summer weather, but should be thoroughly warmed up at the end of the five-mile climb to Stoke summit which lies ahead. Grantham had traditionally been a place where the engines of East Coast expresses were changed but, with many more through workings between London and the North, the practice had declined somewhat at the time of the photograph. Presented to the National Railroad Museum at Green Bay, Wisconsin, USA in April 1964, this is one of the six 'A4s' still in existence.

*Below:* Another 'A4' which has survived into preservation is No 60009 *Union of South Africa*, purchased after withdrawal in June 1966 and shipped to Lochty for private use on the former East Fife Central line, which had been closed to traffic in 1964. She is shown here standing in Perth station in May 1964 while working the 5.30pm from Buchanan Street to Aberdeen. This locomotive was destined to once again work out of King's Cross later that year, hauling the 'Jubilee Requiem' to Newcastle and back. The outward trip was badly delayed but, returning, No 60009 gained 28min on the scheduled time. The square plaque depicting a springbok was donated by a South African newspaper proprietor and is fitted only on the left-hand side of the engine.

*Above: Union of South Africa* was one of the five 'A4s' intended for working the prewar 'Coronation' luxury train, linking London and Edinburgh in a journey time of 6hr, which were given names of constituent countries of the British Commonwealth and Empire. Another of these was *Dominion of Canada* which, apart from a few months in 1957, was allocated to King's Cross from the time of its entering service in 1937 until the motive power depot closed in June 1963. Thereafter, No 60010 was sent to New England depot for a few months before moving on to Ferryhill shed, Aberdeen. The following spring saw her at work on the Glasgow trains, on which she was employed when photographed approaching Perth with the 5.30pm from Buchanan Street. In 1965 she became unfit for service and, after being laid-up for a while, was externally

reconditioned at Crewe Works and presented to the Canadian Historical Railroad Association, leaving Britain in 1967.

*Right: Commonwealth of Australia*, she of the very long nameplate, is seen here working light engine through North Queensferry station, not far from her former home of 26 years at Haymarket shed, Edinburgh. No 60012 was another of those 'A4s' from both north and south of the Border which were to spend their final days at Aberdeen, after the East Coast main line services were fully dieselised in 1963. When photographed, in May 1964, she was to remain in service only a few more months, withdrawal taking place in August.

*Left:* The first four 'A4s' to be built, of which *Quicksilver* was one, were painted to match the silver-grey-liveried 'Silver Jubilee' train, and the theme was extended to the locomotive names, each of which embodied the word 'silver'. The service, which had in 1935 cut the journey time between Newcastle and London to 4hr, ended in 1939 and, with the silver-grey livery having disappeared from the locomotives even earlier, only their names survived the war as a reminder of their original purpose. Of that original quartet of 'A4s', the three based in London appeared most often on the 'Silver Jubilee'. The odd one out, *Silver King*, would usually stand pilot at Newcastle in case the 'Silver Jubilee' booked engine was indisposed, before working a train to Edinburgh once the flyer was safely away. Postwar, she was a noted performer on the up 'Flying Scotsman' between Newcastle and Grantham. In the photograph, with less than a year of life remaining, No 60016 *Silver King* is waiting to take over the Aberdeen portion of the up West Coast postal, which it will work forward to Carstairs.

*Below:* At those times when the main line south of Doncaster was closed due to engineering work, trains would be diverted onto the Lincolnshire loop line through Gainsborough and Lincoln. On such an occasion, and in bitterly cold weather, 'A4' No 60015 *Quicksilver* is at the head of an up express which has just passed Lea Road station, Gainsborough, and is recovering speed after the tortuous crossing of the River Trent. The bridge over the Trent was originally owned by the Manchester, Sheffield & Lincolnshire Railway, the GNR's loop line sharing it with that company's Retford to Gainsborough section.

*Left: Silver Fox*, another of the original batch of 'A4s', on 27 August 1936 captured the world speed record for steam by attaining 113mph. Unfortunately, the locomotive suffered severe internal damage as a result of the effort and finally entered King's Cross station, in the words of Cecil J. Allen who was on the train: '…roaring like a wounded bull…steam shooting straight out at the front end'. In this early 1962 view No 60017, though clearly going quite strongly past Retford, is again in trouble with severe steam leakage at the front end. The misfortune for the photographer was that the leak was on the wrong side of the engine; that of the passengers would be a probable late arrival in London! The flying foxes embellished on both sides of the engine were made and presented by Samuel Fox & Co Ltd, makers of stainless steels.

*Above:* Whether or not *Silver Fox* made it safely to Grantham, here we have an 'A4' that has, hauling the afternoon down Niddrie goods. Though this is the type of employment the 'V2' class 2-6-2s were intended for, this particular express goods train was regularly worked to Newcastle by a King's Cross Pacific which returned with an overnight passenger train. On this occasion, Gateshead's 'A4' No 60019 *Bittern* had the job.

*Above: Bittern*, destined to be one of the last two 'A4s' to remain in service, had by the end of 1963 moved to Ferryhill. When, against all expectations, the 'A4s' continued to work the Glasgow to Aberdeen services in the summer of 1966 she was prominent during the early part of the season on the 8.26am from Glasgow, returning on the 5.15pm from Aberdeen, and is shown here north of Stonehaven on the morning train. Disappointingly, *Bittern* was to be out of traffic for a long period later that summer in spite of having had a major repair as recently as April, but on 3 September she worked an excursion from Glasgow to Aberdeen and back which was advertised as the last public run behind an 'A4'. The return fare was £2 4s 0d (£2.20)! Following official withdrawal later that month, the locomotive was purchased for private preservation but continued to occasionally perform on excursion trains later in the year.

*Right:* No such rites attended the final days of 'A4' No 60025 *Falcon*, one of the victims of the 1963 axe. Already wearing a forlorn look, she is seen in the spring of that year descending Gamston bank with a down express, probably deputising for a diesel, although the train is longer than those normally entrusted to diesels. Four 'A4s' had already gone at the end of 1962 and *Falcon* was to join them before the current year was out.

*Above left:* We flash back to a summer afternoon at Grantham in 1959 and three pictures depicting happier times for the 'A4s', when the 19 allocated to King's Cross shed were fully active. With its valve gear in the full forward position, immaculately clean No 60021 *Wild Swan* moves a southbound express out of the station with apparent ease. When first built, the Gresley Pacifics had their cut-off limited to 65% of the piston stroke in full forward gear, but problems in starting very heavy wartime trains led to this being changed to 75%. All the 'A4s' had been altered by 1957.

*Left:* A little later that same day, the Niddrie goods is seen heading north behind No 60029 *Woodcock*, also in fine fettle.

*Above:* A further example of the superb external condition of the King's Cross top-link Pacifics, right down to polished buffers and drawgear, No 60007

*Sir Nigel Gresley*, is moving on to Grantham shed having just worked a train down from King's Cross. A few weeks earlier this engine had made one of the finest runs ever recorded with an 'A4' when, on 23 May 1959, it headed the Stephenson Locomotive Society's Golden Jubilee tour from King's Cross to Doncaster and back. The normal maximum line speed of 90mph had been relaxed, and the locomotive reached speeds of over 100mph three times in the course of the round trip, including a maximum of 112mph. Perhaps even more impressive was the speed of 82mph attained over Stoke summit on the down run. No 60007 had in April become the first 'A4' to be fitted with a Smith-Stone speed indicator driven, as may be seen in the photograph, from the left-hand trailing crankpin. The instrument probably prompted the official restraining hand that reportedly curtailed the maximum speed the locomotive was allowed to reach on the run mentioned above.

*Below:* The most famous 'A4' of all, No 60022 *Mallard*, is approaching Grantham with an up express. This was one of the four 'A4s' which were fitted with the Kylchap blast pipe and double chimney when first built. There is little doubt that this feature assisted the locomotive in establishing the long-enduring world speed record for steam traction of 126mph, and the improved performance it provided was further acknowledged by the selection of three of the Kylchap-fitted 'A4s' as the ex-LNER representatives in the British Railways 1948 interchange trials. There they had supremacy over all the other types tested in economy of coal and water consumption, so it is all the more surprising that almost a decade was to elapse before the rest of the class received this relatively inexpensive modification.

*Right: Mallard*, as now preserved in the National Railway Museum at York, is the closest of any of the surviving 'A4s' to its original condition, not only in having had the double chimney from new but also in having had the continuous side valances restored, thereby enclosing most of the valve gear. Opinions differ on the aesthetic merits of this, but those for whom an essential part of the attraction of a modern steam locomotive is to see the wheels and valve motion in full view would have rejoiced at the sight of 'A4' No 60025 *Falcon* as she accelerated a down express away from Grantham. In its elegant action a Gresley Pacific's valve gear was truly poetry in motion. These two photographs, taken within minutes of each other — the signals above *Falcon's* second carriage showing line clear for *Mallard* — again bear testimony to the exemplary turnout of Top Shed 'A4s' in the summer of 1962.

*Left:* Based for many years at Haymarket shed, *Kingfisher* was, in September 1965, one of the eight 'A4s' which were concentrated at Aberdeen. At the head of the 1.30pm express from that city No 60024 is running a little early and is awaiting departure time at Dunblane station, from where she will have an easy downhill run to the next stop at Stirling.

*Above:* In May 1966, still employed on the Aberdeen to Glasgow services, *Kingfisher* is seen near Stonehaven. Although to the north of Stonehaven the line is never very far from the East Coast historically it was first and foremost part of the West Coast route to Aberdeen, being owned by the former Caledonian Railway. The East Coast companies only had use of it by virtue of running powers between Kinnaber Junction and Aberdeen. Along with *Bittern*, No 60024 was to be in operation during the final week which saw the end of regular LNER Pacific working on this line.

*Left:* Although allocated to Haymarket shed when new in 1937, then named *Kestrel*, 'A4' No 60026 *Miles Beevor* spent most of the postwar years at King's Cross until that depot closed in 1963. Transferred to St Margaret's later that year and placed in store over the winter, No 60026 returned to service at Ferryhill shed and was put to work on the Aberdeen to Glasgow run. Soon after leaving Perth, *Miles Beevor* is heading the morning express from Aberdeen in May 1964. A short distance ahead the line enters a tunnel, emerging at Hilton Junction where this former LMS West Coast route to Aberdeen is joined from the east by the ex-LNER line from Edinburgh via Glenfarg, which 'A4s' working into Perth in earlier years would have traversed.

*Below:* This view depicts *Miles Beevor*, soon to be withdrawn in December 1965, running above Allan Water, north of Dunblane, with the 5.30pm Glasgow to Aberdeen express in September 1965. After the passage of this train a hasty retreat from this seemingly idyllic location was necessary due to the attentions of swarms of tiny but extremely voracious midges.

*Above left:* The 'Elizabethan' express, which first ran in 1953, continued a tradition of running a daily nonstop run between King's Cross and Edinburgh which had begun in 1928 with the 10am 'Flying Scotsman' service. The practice had been made possible by the use of Gresley's corridor tenders which enabled the engine crew to change places with a relief crew in the train at the halfway point of the journey. By 1954 the journey time had been cut to 6½hr which, with a train weight of over 400 tons, made the task of haulage especially arduous for the 'A4s' which invariably performed it.

*Left:* On Saturdays and Sundays 'The Elizabethan' service did not operate but the locomotives allocated to the duty still worked through between the two capitals, albeit *not* non-stop, hauling the 'Elizabethan' stock on Saturdays and an *ad hoc* formation on Sundays. 'A4' No 60030 *Golden Fleece* is approaching York with the southbound Saturday working in 1961.

*Above:* During the last year of steam working for this train we see No 60028 *Walter K. Whigham*, the locomotive which had taken the first 'Elizabethan' out of King's Cross in 1953, arriving there with the up working in July 1961. The distance of 392¾ miles covered by this train was the longest daily nonstop run in the world but, on the eve of the inauguration of nonstop running in 1928, the LMS had made a pre-emptive one-off run from Euston to Glasgow, 401½ miles nonstop, as a spoiler for the LNER's publicity. That record was not taken back by the LNER until 1948 when flooding on the East Coast main line caused the nonstop 'Flying Scotsman' to be diverted via St Boswells and Kelso, increasing the distance to 408½ miles. The nonstop run was to be achieved 17 times, and on the first occasion the locomotive was *Woodcock*. No 60028's tender is one of the streamlined corridor tenders built specially for the 'A4s' while those attached to Nos 60030 and 60032 opposite, which have beading along the top edge of the sides, originally belonged to 'A3s'.

*Below:* On 29 August 1965, Perth motive power depot was host to four 'A4s': No 60009 *Union of South Africa*, No 60026 *Miles Beevor*, No 60019 *Bittern* and No 60031 *Golden Plover*. The last of these was based at St Rollox and has been given the diagonal yellow stripe which adorned the cabsides of many London Midland Region locomotives which were not permitted to operate under the electric wires south of Crewe.

*Right:* We take leave of the 'A4s' with this shot of the formerly King's Cross-based No 60034 *Lord Farringdon*, departing from Perth with the 7.10am Aberdeen to Glasgow express in September 1965. This was another of the 'A4s' to survive into 1966 and was active at least until the end of May, withdrawal taking place in August.

The first 'A3' Pacific was LNER No 4480 *Enterprise* (pictured on page 3 as No 60111), a rebuild of one of the original batch of LNER 'A1' Pacifics, giving it a higher pressure boiler with a larger superheater. All the 'A1s' were eventually to be similarly altered but, meanwhile, new production 'A3s' were built between 1928 and 1935, of which No 60039 *Sandwich* was one of the last, having been turned out by Doncaster works in 1934. The nameplates of this last batch of nine 'A3s' carried lettering of the Gill Sans Medium type — which was to become standard on LNER straight nameplates — in place of the bolder style of characters hitherto used. A curiosity about this engine at the time was the partial obscurement of the front numberplate by the smokebox handrail, something which was corrected later on. Note also the Automatic Warning System apparatus, seen below the front drawgear, which had begun to be fitted to Pacifics working on the East Coast main line in 1958. *Sandwich* is pictured in April 1959, moving on to Grantham shed having just worked down from King's Cross.

In July 1959 *Sandwich* was to receive a Kylchap blast pipe and double chimney, and the change in appearance which would result is seen in this same-angle view of the already-fitted No 60065 *Knight of Thistle*. Following conversion of all the 'A4s', a start had been made on fitting double chimneys to the remainder of the 'A3s' — *Humorist* having carried one for many years — and all were to be dealt with by early 1960. Without doubt the double chimneys greatly improved the performance of the 'A3s', allowing them to be utilised as the equals of the 'A4s' and the much newer Peppercorn 'A1s' on the most arduous duties, but the view was widely held that the modification marred the appearance of these most beautiful of engines. Mercifully, ugly smoke deflectors of the type carried by *Humorist*, which might have been expected, were absent.

*Left:* The absence of smoke deflectors on the double chimney 'A3s' was, sadly, to be only temporary. The softer blast from the double chimneys increased the effect of the exhaust beating down in certain weather conditions to the detriment of visibility from the cab. The fitting of the hideous, but apparently very effective German-type deflectors overcame the problem but seriously impaired — some would say ruined — the appearance of the locomotives. In the latter respect they are seen to maximum disadvantage in this view of No 60039 *Sandwich*, passing Markham summit with a down express, yet appear to be functioning exactly as intended, although the still air of this March 1963 morning would hardly have provided the stiffest of tests.

*Below:* In the summer of 1962 No 60059 *Tracery*, having been kitted out with deflectors in September 1961 yet destined to remain in service only until the end of 1962, is braking an up express for its stop at Grantham. The junction in the foreground is the divergence of the Grantham to Nottingham line which continues parallel to the main lines as far as the next signalbox, Barrowby Road, before swinging away westwards. In LNER days the line carried a short-lived Pullman service to Nottingham and Sheffield, but was now used only by a sparse service of stopping trains.

*Above:* Standing pilot at Grantham shed early in 1959, well-groomed 'A3' No 60047 *Donovan* still has its single chimney, as well as the earlier style of round dome which was a characteristic of the Diagram 94 HP boilers fitted to the original 'A3s'. A banjo-shaped steam collector was provided on the boilers of the last batch of 'A3s' and this boiler type gradually came to be fitted to most members of the class, there being very few 94 HP boilers remaining by the 1960s.

*Right:* On her next overhaul at Doncaster works a few weeks later, *Donovan* was fitted with one of the later Diagram 94A boilers, as well as receiving the Kylchap blast pipe and double chimney. In July 1959 she is seen arriving at Grantham shed after travelling, light engine, from the north. To judge from the external condition, newly painted but dusty from running-in duties, this was probably her delivery back into traffic following the works visit.

*Left:* Locomotives were turned at Grantham on a triangle situated on the western side of the shed, and therefore invisible from the station and the main line. 'A3' No 60048 *Doncaster* is backing towards the first reversing point at the extreme right of the photograph. After traversing the next side of the triangle chimney-first, she will reverse along the line from which the photograph is taken before crossing the line she now occupies. This was a curious layout, but excellent for securing multiple shots of engines turning!

*Below:* While many of the Pacific diagrams from King's Cross involved the engine in returning home the following day, there were also 'day-return' workings to Grantham. Employed on one of these, No 60044 *Melton* is making ready for the second leg of her duty at Grantham, with the efforts of the fireman very much in evidence. This locomotive was the first of the batch of 20 'A1s' built at Doncaster in 1924-5 and was not rebuilt to 'A3' until 1947. A much transferred engine, she spent her last six years at King's Cross depot, lasting until June 1963.

*Above:* 'A3' No 60050 *Persimmon*, from New England shed, is breasting Markham summit with an up express on a foggy morning early in 1963. *Persimmon* is remembered as one of the three members of the class, the others being *Blink Bonny* and *Enterprise*, which operated from Neasden shed on the former Great Central line for several years in the early 1950s. Despite the dirty external appearance, the locomotive appears to be on song here but was to survive in service only a few more months, being withdrawn in June 1963.

*Right:* 'A3' No 60105 *Victor Wild*, a Grantham-based engine for the last 12 years of its life, is seen at its home depot in 1962. As LNER No 4474, one of the batch of 10 'A1s' built in 1923-4, the engine was notable in having participated in the interchange trials with the GWR in 1925. Operating on the GWR in competition with that company's No 4074 *Caldicot Castle*, the LNER engine came off second-best, consuming 6lb per mile more coal than its rival on the trial runs. A similar contest on LNER metals between No 4475 and GWR No 4079 also concluded in the GWR's favour. Two years were to pass before the LNER arrived at a satisfactory valve gear design which reduced the Pacifics' coal consumption by over 10lb per mile. How interesting a repeat would have been of the competition with *Victor Wild*, as depicted here in its final condition, and *Caldicot Castle* when that engine was 'modernised', late in *its* life, with double chimney and four-row superheater!

*Below:* The worn condition of Grantham 'A3' No 60056 *Centenary's* paintwork would suggest that a general repair is imminent, as might the humble duty the locomotive is performing: that of hauling the 4.45pm all stations to Peterborough, whose empty stock she is bringing out of the sidings in May 1959. *Centenary* and *Prince of Wales* were two of the handful of 'A3s' which were not named after racehorses. *Centenary* was so named because it was the first locomotive built at Doncaster works in 1925, when the railway centenary celebrations took place, and LNER No 2553, originally named *Manna*, was in 1926 renamed after the Prince of Wales who had inspected the locomotive on a recent visit to Doncaster works.

*Right:* No 60054 *Prince of Wales* was another of the 'A3s' which had a long postwar spell on the Great Central section, at Leicester shed, returning to the GN main line in 1956. Early in 1959, newly fitted with a double chimney and in better external condition than the author ever remembers her on the GC, No 60054 heads south from Grantham into a gathering storm in April 1959.

*Left:* Excluding the solitary long-time example of *Humorist*, the first 'A3' to receive a double chimney was No 60055 *Woolwinder* in June 1958, at the start of the programme which would result in the entire class of 78 engines being converted by January 1960. Contrary to some accounts which credit Doncaster with the initiative for this policy, P. N. Townend, in his very informative book *Top Shed*, reveals that it was repeated requests from King's Cross motive power depot, against a degree of resistance from the CME's department, which led to the conversions. Certainly, Top Shed made good use of its Kylchap 'A3s', of which *Woolwinder* was one. At the age of 35 years, in one 11-day period in 1960, this engine reportedly covered over 4,000 miles on top-link duties. She was photographed passing Grove Road, south of Retford, with an up Newcastle express in early 1959.

*Above:* Going south from Retford, the GN main line rises on a 1 in 178/200 gradient for five miles to a summit point at Markham before descending into the Trent Valley at Newark. This was a stiff climb for trains restarting from Retford but for nonstop trains, passing the station at up to 80mph, it provided only a moderate check in speed. In June 1960, recently ex-works 'A3' No 60085 *Manna* is about halfway up the climb, at Eaton Wood. In the distance, the line takes a wide curve to the left before disappearing off the edge of the picture, at which point the photograph opposite was taken.

*Left:* At Retford the Great Northern main line made a level crossing of the Manchester, Sheffield & Lincolnshire Railway and it is over that crossing that 'A3' No 60065 *Knight of Thistle* is hauling a northbound express goods train. It is a sad reality that in the twilight years of steam, the Pacifics were increasingly to be seen on such inappropriate duties. Since the photograph reproduced on page 31 was taken, the locomotive has had a boiler change, acquiring in 1960 the Diagram 94 HP type it was to carry until withdrawal in 1964. A strange fact is that the engine was named *Knight of the Thistle*, after the racehorse which won the 1897 Royal Hunt Cup, until 1932 when new nameplates were fitted omitting 'the' from the name. This is believed to have been an error but it was never corrected. The signals behind the station wall guard the crossing from the east whence, before the direct line was opened, the GNR's through traffic would have come. The wall itself is host to the usual band of loco-spotters which regularly congregated here.

*Below:* On 15 March 1959, 'A3' No 60062 *Minoru* is standing at Retford station with the 10.35am Leeds to King's Cross express. The locomotive appears to be in superb condition having had a general repair, including the fitting of a double chimney, in the previous month. During her 39 years of service, almost 25 of which were at King's Cross shed, *Minoru* was reallocated no less than 17 times, finally being withdrawn from New England in December 1964.

*Below:* All except 20 Gresley Pacifics were constructed at Doncaster works, the exceptions being a batch of the early 'A1s' which were built in Glasgow by the North British Locomotive Co in 1924. These engines were based exclusively in the northern areas of the LNER for many years, but in 1950 four of them — *Tagalie, Knight of Thistle, Merry Hampton* and *Ladas* — were transferred south from Haymarket in exchange for *Felstead, Papyrus, Humorist* and *Spion Kop.* The reason for the transfers seems to have been that the Haymarket engines, though already converted to 'A3s', still had the driving position on the right-hand side of the cab as they were originally built as 'A1s', whereas the engines sent north were first built as 'A3s' which had been designed with left-hand drive — a feature greatly preferred by the Scottish enginemen. Two of the

locomotives transferred south are pictured in 1962, both long since converted to left-hand drive. No 60067 *Ladas* is wheeling an up express into Grantham.

*Right:* Slowed by signals, No 60066 *Merry Hampton* is also approaching Grantham with a down train. This engine, uniquely, has a higher than normal cab ventilator, a relic of earlier days when the first 'A1s' had the higher cabs and boiler mountings afforded by the generous GNR loading gauge. When the engines were later made to conform to the overall LNER loading gauge the cabs were lowered, along with all the ventilators except the one on this cab, which originally belonged to LNER No 4481 *St Simon.*

*Left:* The 'Queen of Scots' all-Pullman train first ran in 1928 connecting London and Glasgow via Leeds, Newcastle and Edinburgh, a distance of 450½ miles. There was a reversal at Leeds necessitating an engine change, and in BR days the usual motive power between Leeds and Newcastle in both directions were Neville Hill 'A3s' which also had charge of the opposite direction 'North Briton' Leeds to Glasgow trains to balance up their day. In the spring of 1959 the down train is seen near Harrogate headed by double chimney 'A3' No 60081 *Shotover*. This was one of the five 'A1s' that had been converted to 'A3' in 1927-8, well before the rest which were not dealt with until the war years and beyond.

*Above:* The last 'A3' to run without smoke deflectors was No 60075 *St Frusquin* and, though the locomotive survived into 1964, they were never fitted. *St Frusquin* is carrying an 'A4' boiler, which has a shorter barrel than the usual 'A3' type and is recognisable in having the rearmost boiler band positioned further forward than normal in relation to the firebox. The 'banjo' dome is also further forward but this is scarcely discernible. When fitted to 'A3s' these boilers, normally operating at 250lb/sq in, had the pressure reduced to 220lb/sq in. Temporarily allocated to Darlington, whose Pacifics did little other than stand pilot in case of failures, she is probably deputising for a failed diesel when photographed at Grantham in 1962.

*Above;* All except five 'A3s' were named after racehorses, usually winners of one or more of the classic races. Two exceptions have been mentioned; the others were *Sir Frederick Banbury*, *Flying Scotsman* and, probably, *Dick Turpin* — although this certainly has equine connections. Freshly outshopped following heavy overhaul at Doncaster Works, No 60080 *Dick Turpin* was photographed at Doncaster motive power depot in March 1958. At that time No 60080 was allocated to Heaton shed and had spent all her working life there, apart from a short spell at neighbouring Gateshead.

*Left:* The nameplate shows the style of lettering applied to most of the class and is typical in spanning the whole arc of the splasher irrespective of the length of the name, though some of the earlier engines did have shorter plates, if the name allowed — *Flying Fox* and *Minoru*, for example.

*Above:* The majority of the North British-built engines were allocated to North Eastern depots. Nicely groomed No 60082 *Neil Gow*, portrayed here filling the tender tank at York shed in 1959, was another of the Geordie Pacifics. The first 52 Gresley Pacifics had tenders of the type fitted to No 60082. Holding 5,000gal of water and 8 tons of coal they were of traditional GNR appearance with rounded corners and coal rails, but had eight wheels and a rigid wheelbase of 16ft which initially raised fears of possible derailments in the cramped confines of locomotive yards and sidings.

*Right:* The name commemorates the winner of the 2,000 Guineas in 1910. Does it matter whether anybody remembered this event in 1925 when the locomotive was new? Some of the other names had their origins even further back, but were more topical on the later engines — *Windsor Lad* entered service in 1934, the year its namesake won the Derby and St Leger. Few would deny that, on the whole, the 'A3s' were fortunate in having such a wonderfully diverse and harmonious collection of names. Note the cast plate on *Neil Gow's* splasher on which can be discerned the locomotive's LNER number: 2581.

*Below:* Arguably the most famous LNER Pacific was No 4472 *Flying Scotsman*, the first turned out by the LNER and the first to attain a speed of 100mph. Having received one of the newly built corridor tenders, No 4472 hauled the first nonstop 'Flying Scotsman' on 1 May 1928, a feat which it was to repeat exactly 40 years later when in private ownership. As No 60103, and coupled to one of the streamlined non-corridor tenders provided for the 'A3s' when their corridor tenders were removed to the 'A4s', the celebrated locomotive is in her final British Railways guise and is shown easing a down express into Grantham in June 1962. Despite the ex-works condition displayed here, she would be withdrawn from service less than a year later, making her official last run on 14 January 1963. Although this locomotive was, incredibly, not among those scheduled for official preservation, it has survived in private hands despite being in peril on the seas, or over the seas, too many times.

*Right:* Another 'A3' which had spent its entire life working from Tyneside was No 60085 *Manna* ('*Manna* from Heaton!' was the gricers' cry) seen entering Grantham station with an up express on 23 May 1959. Although Pacifics from Heaton would often be replaced by another engine here — removing to the running shed where the fire would be cleaned and the tender replenished to make ready for the return trip to Newcastle a few hours later — on this occasion No 60085 continued southwards. The engine, the second to be named *Manna*, had carried the name since entering service in 1930. Earlier, the name belonged to 'A1' No 2553.

*Left:* Though *Flying Scotsman* is the longest-lived LNER Pacific, *Flying Fox* had the longest record in service, with 41 years 8 months to her credit, clocking up over 2.6 million miles. The redoubtable *Tracery* was not far behind, with 2.5 million miles, and three others exceeded 2.25 million. No 60106, seen on shed at Grantham, was in the course of a six-year spell there when these photographs were taken, her longest anywhere apart from the 14 years at King's Cross from entering service in 1923.

*Below:* No 60106 is in full flight approaching Grantham with an up express in 1962. Withdrawal of this grand old engine took place at the end of 1964, in which year she was recorded as having attained 98mph on a Gresley Society special, and on other occasions as having almost succeeded in maintaining 'Deltic' schedules when called upon in an emergency.

*Left:* 'A3' No 60111 *Enterprise* is leaving York in October 1959 with a King's Cross to Newcastle boat train. This engine has one of the high-sided non-corridor tenders which were first fitted to those 'A3s' built from 1930 onwards. Similar to the original corridor tenders in external appearance, though slightly narrower, they had the same capacity, 5,000gal of water and 9 tons of coal. In later years the tenders were frequently interchanged between locomotives, *Enterprise* acquiring this one in 1938.

*Above:* Edward Thompson had already brought out two versions of his mixed-traffic 'A2' Pacifics when he turned his attention to producing a new standard express passenger Pacific designated Class A1 (the original 'A1s' had been reclassified 'A10'). The stated intention was that the new design would be based on the existing 'A4' but, when it emerged, there was little resemblance to the 'A4s', the layout owing more to Thompson's new 'A2s'. Though nominally a rebuild of the original 'A1' *Great Northern* of 1922, so little of this remained after the rebuilding that the whole exercise was tantamount to scrapping the historic Gresley locomotive and appropriating its name. An important consideration had been the elimination of the Gresley conjugated valve gear for the inside cylinder, which had become more troublesome due to declining standards of maintenance. This meant dividing the drive between the two leading coupled axles, but the method Thompson so admired on GWR four-cylinder locomotives led, in this case, to a massive and ungainly elongation of the front end of the new Pacific. As a one-off the locomotive, not surprisingly, spent a lot of time under repair but when based at Doncaster late in its life, and now reclassified 'A1/1', No 60113 was often seen on express passenger workings to London such as the one recorded leaving Retford in the late 1950s.

*Below:* When the new standard 'A1' came into production it was, unlike *Great Northern*, recognisable as a descendant of the Gresley Pacifics. It adhered to the more compact layout A. H. Peppercorn had adopted in his version of the 'A2' class introduced in the preceding year. The new locomotives were immediately employed on the more arduous haulage tasks, releasing some of the older Pacifics and the 'V2' 2-6-2s on to lesser duties. Entering Grantham with a down Leeds and Bradford express is Copley Hill's No 60117 *Bois Roussel*, built at Doncaster in 1948.

*Right:* The same engine is seen storming over Markham summit with a southbound express in 1963. *Bois Roussel*, withdrawn in 1965 with less than 17 years of service to its credit, would have given a good many more but for the obsessively hasty and ill-considered railway dieselisation programme.

*Left:* Inside York shed in October 1964 are 'A1s' No 60146 *Peregrine* and No 60121 *Silurian*, the latter being one of three members of this class to spend their entire working lives allocated there.

*Below:* On the same day the other roundhouse at York held 'A1' No 60124 *Kenilworth*, seen here in company with 'V2' 2-6-2s Nos 60876 and 60963. Both the 'V2s' had been altered from their original condition, No 60876 in having independent cylinder castings and outside steam pipes, while No 60963 had been given a Kylchap blast pipe and double chimney. Seven of the 'A1s', including this one, eventually took names which were formerly carried by 'Scott' class 4-4-0 engines. In this case the 'D30' continued to run for several years still bearing its name, an odd situation when other genuinely redundant — and wonderfully resonant — names could have been chosen from the same source. Looking at this smoky interior, would anyone have imagined that one day it would become the Great Hall of the National Railway Museum?

*Above:* When the 'A1s' were first introduced, York motive power depot had an initial allocation of only six but, as dieselisation progressed, the class tended to gravitate northwards so that by 1964 this had grown to a dozen or so, for which there seemed to be little or no express passenger work other than in deputising for failed diesels. In April 1965 No 60138 *Boswell*, another of those lifelong York 'A1s', is in company with No 60155 *Borderer* in the yard at York.

*Right:* Later in their lives some of the 'A1s' were fitted with boilers originally provided for the Thompson 'A2/3' Pacifics, recognisable by having the dome positioned on the second boiler band. No 60125 *Scottish Union* had been one of the recipients when photographed near Grantham in 1962 and was to carry this boiler until being scrapped in July 1964. These boilers were of the round-dome type, but dummy banjo-dome covers were usually fitted.

*Above:* The 'A1s' are credited with having been the most reliable of all LNER Pacifics, recorded as averaging over 100,000 miles between general repairs, and having the highest availability for traffic. The only criticism to be frequently voiced was that the class as a whole tended to be rough riders, inhibiting drivers from running really fast, though this is confounded by recorded instances of 'A1s' reaching speeds in excess of 100mph. When this photograph of No 60140 *Balmoral* was taken in 1962, the first withdrawal of an 'A1' had just occurred and four more were to be taken out of service before the end of the year.

*Right:* The distinction of being the last 'A1' to remain in service fell to No 60145 *Saint Mungo,* seen at York in April 1965 in excellent external condition. First withdrawn from Darlington shed in March 1966 along with No 60124, she was later reinstated at York before being finally withdrawn in June 1966. *Saint Mungo* had been one of the last 'A1s' to receive a general repair, fittingly at Darlington Works, as she was one of the 23 engines of the class (Nos 60130 to 60152) which were originally constructed there. The electric lights, with which the class were originally fitted and which most were to retain, have been removed from this locomotive, to the benefit of its appearance.

*Left:* Shorn of nameplates and reminiscent of the early days of the class when they ran without names, No 60151 is at York in August 1965 when newly transferred there from Gateshead. Despite the splendid external condition she was not to last the year out, being withdrawn from York in November. The name formerly carried by this engine, *Midlothian*, was one of seven names inherited by 'A1s' from the ex-NBR Atlantics which had been scrapped in the 1930s.

*Below:* Another of those ex-Atlantic names was *Bon Accord*, still carried by No 60154 when at York in the autumn of 1964. This was one of five 'A1s' experimentally fitted with Timken roller bearings on all axles when the locomotives were almost new. The roller bearings had the effect of increasing by about 20% the already high mileages covered by the 'A1s' between general repairs, so it is surprising that no further 'A1s' or other Pacifics were fitted, especially as the engines involved in the experiment retained the roller bearings to the end. When the 'A1s' were at their peak in pre-diesel days, Nos 60154 and 60155 from Gateshead shed are recorded as having had, for several years, a virtual monopoly of the 'Night Scotsman' through workings to King's Cross.

*Left:* The changing fortunes of the 'A1s' are reflected in these two photographs. From the time when the 'A1s' were at their peak comes this view of No 60128 *Bongrace* storming away from Retford with the 10am Leeds to King's Cross. Top Shed was to lose the last of its 'A1s', including *Bongrace*, in April 1959.

*Above:* Withdrawal was only two months away for No 60152 *Holyrood* when photographed in the repair shop at York in April 1965. This engine had only come to York the previous year, after spending all its earlier working life in the Scottish Region. The electric light generator can be clearly seen in this view, tucked under the smokebox above the oil lamp. In spite of the electric lights, display of oil lamps was still obligatory for train identification during the hours of daylight.

*Left:* Edward Thompson's first 4-6-2 engines appeared in 1943 in the form of a rebuild of the six Class P2 'Mikados' that Gresley had designed specifically for the heavily graded Edinburgh to Aberdeen route. Their clumsy appearance, with outside cylinders to the rear of the bogie rather than astride it, could perhaps be attributed to wartime stringencies requiring the use of as much of the original locomotives as possible, which in the event must have been very little indeed. That view is not borne out by the fact that Thompson used the same layout on all his subsequent Pacifics where such constraints did not apply. The inside cylinder, pushed well forward, drove the leading coupled axle in similar fashion to the Great Western four-cylinder 4-6-0s, but it was the resultant lengthening of the front end and the enormous smokebox together with the empty expanse above the bogie, that contributed most to the locomotive's uncouth appearance. The rebuilds, which eventually came to be classified as 'A2/2', were returned to Scotland where they were often employed on express goods and fish trains. In 1949 the whole class was transferred south, divided between York and New England, in an Anglo-Scottish exchange which took six Peppercorn 'A2s' north of the Border. Ten years later No 60501 *Cock o' the North*, having by then received a standard Peppercorn Pacific boiler which had resulted in modification to the original V-shaped cab front, moves off Grantham shed to work back home to York.

*Right:* Another early 1959 shot shows *Cock o' the North* having just passed through the short Askham Tunnel, south of Retford, with a down express. Withdrawal of the class began in November 1959 and was complete in July 1961, No 60501 lasting until February 1960.

*Above:* When Thompson produced his standard mixed-traffic Pacific in 1946 it closely resembled the rebuilds of the 2-8-2s in its unorthodox layout, although very large platform-mounted smoke deflectors had replaced the small smokebox wing plates which had proved ineffective at lifting the smoke on the earlier engines. Eventually classified 'A2/3', they possessed a fair turn of speed despite their smaller wheels, and the cramped valve gear contributed to the impression of hustle they often created. A rather unkempt member of the class, No 60522 *Straight Deal*, is speeding through Ordsall, Retford on a bright morning in 1962. Having spent much of its life allocated to York motive power depot, No 60522 was soon to be transferred to the Scottish Region, putting in another 2½ years

service there. Along with No 60512, this was one of the last two survivors of this class of 15 engines when the pair were withdrawn in June 1965.

*Right:* 'A2/3' No 60513 *Dante* is pictured in rather better external condition than her sister engine. Though originally built with round-dome Diagram 117 boilers, later interchanges with Peppercorn 'A2s' led to some 'A2/3s', including the two examples here, carrying the Diagram 118 type with banjo dome. With these engines the practice of naming after successful racehorses was resumed. *Dante* having won the 1945 Derby, this was a topical choice for LNER No 513, built in 1946.

*Left:* When A. H. Peppercorn became CME of the LNER he at once produced a mixed-traffic Pacific more conventional in outward appearance than those of his predecessor. Divided drive was retained, but the slavish adherence to equal connecting-rod lengths was abandoned. Consequently, the cylinders were once more astride the bogie and the smokebox was of more normal proportions with, surprisingly, a single-chimney exhaust. Fifteen of these 'A2s' were built in 1947-8, the last of which was provided with a Kylchap double chimney, as also were five of the others later on. When first new, five were allocated to the Eastern Region, nine to the North Eastern Region and only one to the Scottish Region, but by 1950 Scotland had the lion's share with 11, only one then remaining on the Eastern Region. No 60528 *Tudor Minstrel*, which had spent most of its days as a Dundee engine, was coasting down to Burntisland with the 12.10pm Dundee to Millerhill express goods train when photographed on 28 August 1965.

*Below:* With Dundee's steeples and chimneys in the background, 'A2s' No 60528 *Tudor Minstrel* and No 60530 *Sayajirao* are seen in the yard at Tay Bridge motive power depot.

*Left:* By August 1965 only three 'A2s' remained in service, all working from Dundee shed. Their duties were mainly on express goods trains with only occasional passenger turns, but on the last two days of the month No 60530 *Sayajirao* was put to work on the 10am Dundee to Glasgow, returning with the 6.15pm from Buchanan Street. With Allan Water in the foreground she is seen climbing towards Kinbuck, north of Dunblane, just before sunset on 30 August 1965.

*Above:* Eastern Region's solitary 'A2' No 60533 *Happy Knight* has just suffered a signal check south of Retford. In its 15-year life this locomotive covered only 800,000 miles and was transferred between depots 12 times. This was one of the five 'A2s' rebuilt in 1949 with double chimneys and multiple-valve regulators. The latter was situated in the superheater header with the associated housing visible behind the chimney, while the rodding which operated the regulator can be seen on the side of the boiler.

*Above:* The last LNER Pacific to remain in service was 'A2' No 60532 *Blue Peter*, which is shown climbing up to the Tay Bridge with the 12.10pm Dundee to Millerhill express goods in September 1965. The withdrawal from service of No 60532 at the end of 1966 brought to an end the 45-year epoch of a great family of engines and closed a memorable chapter in British locomotive history. Fortunately, *Blue Peter* has survived and is preserved in working order.

*Right:* Another view of one of the last survivors, 'A2' No 60530 *Sayajirao*, at Dundee shed. Towards the end of its life this and two other 'A2s' were transferred to the former LMS shed at Polmadie to replace, on the main line to Carlisle, LMS Pacifics which were being withdrawn. Railway loyalties being what they were, it was not surprising that they were not popular, nor that the move was short-lived. No 60530 came to Dundee in July 1964, remaining there until withdrawn in November 1966, only one month before *Blue Peter*.

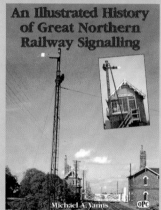